Care of The Senses

By

**Cheryl Sanders Sardello, Ph.D., and
Robert Sardello, Ph.D.**

Table Of Content

INTRODUCTION

"What are our senses?"

In this writing, you will find a description of not just the five senses we are all familiar with - touch, smell, taste, vision and hearing, but on top of these, it describes seven more. It describes how we have senses that tell us something about our own body, where it begins and ends, how it feels, how it moves, and how it can be still, so that we can orientate towards the world around us. Then it describes the four senses with which we explore that surrounding world, and how we can find out about the qualities of all we see, taste, smell and feel. The last four senses develop out of transformation of our healthy body senses and become our social senses, they help us to understand what it is someone is trying to tell us, and through that, who this other person is and how we can connect with the people around us, sense who they really are.

The intention Cheryl and I had when writing this view of senses, strongly influenced by the Spiritual Science of Rudolf Steiner, however, goes considerably beyond broadening what we know as the senses. Each of the senses is described carefully, experientially, and, as you will notice right away, with a high degree of alarm that the very basis of our bodily being is so rapidly eroding. The erosion of sensing within the wholeness of Earth and Cosmos, the concentration on sensation as 'sensational' rather than the inherent spiritual nature of sensing, practically means that there's no here 'here'. We live now, more and more isolated from ongoing bodily engagement with others. The reason, in large part, is the digitalizing of the world, and as our bodies become more and more like 'foreign objects', the center of bodily being, the heart, and thus, love, moves further and further into being mental distance, accompanied by steadily increasing impulses, anxiety and fear. We hope this writing can awaken the countercurrent, the refolding of the human being into the cosmic heartbeat of Love. All of Spiritual Psychology as practiced by our School of Spiritual Psychology has this concern.

Cheryl Sanders Sardello, &Robert Sardello,

Orientation for Considering the Senses

In this monograph, we want to recover neglected dimensions of sensing as integral to being fully human. We propose to do this by means of a careful study of the body in its living relationship with the world. Our approach is founded on a synthesis of three streams of modern psychology: existential phenomenological psychology; C. G. Jung's archetypal psychology of the soul; and psychological contributions found in the spiritual science of Rudolf Steiner, the founder of spiritual science, which he termed Anthroposophy.

Existential phenomenological psychology contributes an important method of describing the human being as what Maurice Merleau-Ponty a significant philosopher in this tradition calls the *body subject*. By this term, he conveys an understanding of the human body as that mysterious and multifaceted phenomenon that always

1

accompanies one's awareness, and indeed, appears to be the very location of consciousness, both of oneself and the world. Merleau-Ponty 's vivid descriptions of the life of embodiment cut through the legacy of Cartesian dualism, and of approaching the mind as if it were not embodied and behavior as if it occurred apart from consciousness (soul).

Jung's psychology which he calls a phenomenology of soul life contributes two important premises to this writing. First, he teaches us to value the inner life and gives a method for doing so objectively by his phenomenology of the soul (or *psyche*), which includes more than subjective awareness; furthermore, he does not divide the soul from the body. He sees soul life as a continuum ranging from instinct to archetype. Second, Jung provides a sensibility for the pathological; if we enter his work carefully, we develop a capacity of knowing when soul is dangerously out of balance.

Rudolf Steiner figures centrally in this writing as the individual who for the first time described twelve senses. He presents these descriptions in numerous places but always as brief indications, which we develop much more extensively here. Through his spiritual science, Steiner also gives an understanding of the human being as a being of body, soul, and spirit; and that understanding also guides the present work.

We hope to show how a convergence of three worldviews enable us to lend deep attention to the obvious, and seeking ways of caring for the senses as a work of self-education. We do not propose a new program but instead hope to open the way for research and observation, which must begin with coming to our senses. It is possible to develop the capacity for creative and profoundly new thinking, through an understanding of the human being and the senses through which we come to perceive the world and others.

First, the present conception of the senses is generally limited to the five or seven most commonly known and typically discounted as mere physical functions rather than soul/spirit activities. The nature of the senses lends them to be overlooked and taken merely as the background of perceiving. There are at least twelve senses serving as the basis through which we can enter the world and participate with the unfolding marvels that are its wonders. Sensing plunges us every moment into delights and distractions, horrors and homeliness. To begin to understand the nature of the sea of sensation in which we swim, the senses must be taken out of their usual nexus of interrelation and interdependence and viewed individually in their uniqueness.

Without a capacity to recognize the full range of the sensory world, we have no proper medium to develop thinking in good directions because then the body is always under stress, though we are not directly conscious of that state. We express ourselves through our bodies first. In the world in which we live today, sensory life is culturally disordered, and we seek more avenues for intensifying physical awareness, whether through drugs, food, exercise, television, or any other of the myriad addictions which increase daily.

In any discussion of the senses we must account for how, out of this array of twelve senses, we experience a unified world. While one sense at a time can be paid attention to, in our ordinary, everyday experience, all of the senses work together giving us the world in a unified manner. We take in the world through touch, balance, smell, taste and all the other senses without having to then make a judgment that there is a unified world out there, whole and complete. A physiologist would say that the brain, acting as a computer, puts all the impressions together into a whole experience. However, even if the brain could do this, it would not account for the experience of perceiving the world, because neither computers nor brains experience anything. If we picture the twelve senses arranged around the circumference of a circle, it is as if something circulates around the circumference, creating a whole out of the twelve parts. Further, we cannot say that this something unifies the impressions of the senses, but rather detects the unity underlying the varied senses, the unity of the surrounding world. The world is already whole and complete; it is not bits and pieces of sense data.

Each sense responds to one aspect of the world - the sound, or the light and color, or the warmth of the world, but each aspect is part of a whole. The inner capacity of experiencing the unified aspect of each of the varied senses is the human spirit, our I being. The conception of the human being as body, soul, and spirit intertwined with the world, differs from the thinking about the nature of the human being modeled on the computer, or the accumulation of information that dismembers perceptions into bits of data.

The senses become disordered when too much of an artificially simulated world inserts itself between our body and the natural world. Through sensing, we open to the vast expanses of the world, from what is at hand, to the outer reaches of the cosmos, and gradually discover ourselves as citizens of Earth. Our senses are disordered at the present time because a simulated world has replaced our surroundings, encasing us in a world of humanly constructed objects of every type, which alters our experience from that of sensing the wholeness of the world to being overwhelmed by sensory objects oriented toward capturing our attention. If our senses do not give us the real qualities of the outer world, we become surrounded by materialized representations of the world.

By way of example, taking each sense individually, we find the following alterations of experience:

- The sense of Touch; plastics of all kinds for convenience, synthetic fibers chemically treated, stain and wear resistant fibers in clothing, carpeting and bedclothes, glass, rubber, pressed wood, wallboard; very different from wool, silk, natural wood, soil, stones, skin.

- The sense of Balance; amusement park rides, airplanes, the subway, balancing an infant on its feet because it flexes its muscles when placed in such a position; very different from moving in a natural landscape, standing upright and finding one's balance in one's own time as a baby.

- The sense of Movement; riding in cars, buses,
  airplanes, exercise equipment, modern dances,
  competitive contact sports, power walking for
  fitness or weight loss; very different from going
  for a stroll, riding a bicycle, tai chi, folk
  dancing, watching the movements of clouds,
  water, wheat in a field on a windy day.

- The Life sense; feeling bloated, heavy,
  drugged, bored, stuffed, heartburn, achy, itchy
  all over, weighed down by everything;
  very different from feeling tired, comfortable,
  thirsty, alert, hungry, energetic.

- The Vision sense; Technicolor movies,
  advertising, and billboards, pictures in
  magazines, color television, painted walls;
  very different from the red and orange glow at
  dawn, the purple of the clouds at sunset, the
  play of light and shadow in the forest or off of
  plants.

- The sense of Smell; the odors of cologne,
  artificial scents added to soap, shampoos,

deodorants, toothpaste, powder, crayons, paper, pictures in books ("scratch 'n sniff") chemical pollutants in the air, water, and food, pesticides, exhaust fumes;

very different from the smell of grass, flowers, the human body, puppy's breath, home baked anything.

- The sense of Taste; artificial flavoring in food, canned or processed foods, soft drinks, additives to all food, designer coffee, excessive use of processed salt;

  very different from the taste of fresh fruits, vegetables, water, milk.

- The sense of Warmth; automobiles and homes and public building air conditioning and heating in temperature controlled environments;

  very different from experiencing the changing heat of the seasons, sweating when it's hot, bundling up to go out in winter.

- The sense of Hearing; electronically amplified music, digital recordings, cellular telephones, television, the noise of city and traffic, sirens, horns;
  very different from live music and singing without amplification, conversation, silence.

- The sense of Speech; television, radio, talk shows, specialized technical language, films, degradation of language into slang and mumbled epitaphs, trash novels;
  very different from a conversation, searching for the exact right word, careful description, thoughtful responsiveness.

- The sense of Thought; computers, internet, faxes, teaching information only, television talk shows, learning from a computer, lecturing to an overlarge class, corporate business communication; very different from thinking through ideas in original ways with others, creative thought, teaching out of deeply knowing the nature of one's subject, so that thought imbues one's teaching with originality.

10

- The sense of the I; appealing to the masses, the corporate world, uniformity, conformity, political edicts, mass communications, television, films, peer pressure; very different from perceiving what is unique about an individual, face to face contact, selflessness, interest in the other person.

As we examine the way the senses are forced to operate in the present world, it might seem that a negative stance is being taken toward the whole world, that it might seem that to be healthy it is necessary to isolate ourselves and our children from the influences of the world. But such a conclusion would be deceptive. It is not possible to be in the world without being a part of everything that makes the world what it is. The response is not one of isolation out of fear, but instead, of education toward balance.

Trying to assure a balance in the sensory world, of the mediated with the natural, the simulated with the immediate, constitutes an ongoing self education of the whole human being. We must become aware when the senses, and therefore the perceptions and experiences, are disrupted and are going to continue to be disturbed by the simulated world of technology, science, and economic pursuit, and therefore must be attended to with conscious, fully awakened attention. Balance, and thus freedom of thought and action can be consciously sought and taught, but it cannot occur naturally, particularly as more people live in areas of high population and as technical devices of every sort intervene in our sensory contact with the world.

Understanding the senses goes more deeply when approached in an order given by their characteristics. There are three groupings of the senses, with four senses clustering in each of the three groups. *There are the senses through which we experience our own embodiment or corporeality. They are the senses of touch, balance, movement, and life. Then there are the senses through which we experience the outer world surrounding our body; sight, smell, taste, and warmth. Finally, there are the senses through*

12

which we experience the life of the spirit in the world and others around us; hearing, the speech sense, the thought sense and the sense of the I.

The Corporeal Senses: Description, Imbalances and Healing

The Four Corporeal Senses

Beginning with the senses through which we experience the corporeality of the human body, we recognize that sensing our own bodily life is crucial. Disruption in these senses results in becoming numb to physical feeling, or the immediate feeling of being alive. Although the word "feeling" does signify that feeling correlates to the emotional feeling life as well, the description of these senses will be from the body's perspective. Each of the four corporeal senses gives us the feeling of living in different aspects.

The healthy operation of these senses is responsible for the right working of the will. By 'will' we mean the capacity to meet the world, to encounter it out of the individual forces of bodily life, to move out into the world to find our place, but in such a manner that we respond to what the world presents, not merely what we want to get from it. Since our

14

corporeal body is the aspect of the outer world that is closest to soul's function of picturing the surrounding world as an inner experience, if the corporeal senses are chaotic, become disrupted, confused, distorted, we are in chaotic relation with the world. This fundamental disruption underlies the epidemic of depression, anxiety, and inertia, and thus an inability to meet the world due to a defeated will. If the corporeal senses become imbalanced in childhood, in later life these psychological disorders are particularly difficult to reach due to a misunderstanding of their origins. Because sensory imbalances are particularly dire in the realm of the corporeal senses, sections on those imbalances are given particular attention.

The "life sense" senses the interior conditions of the organs of the body. When the organs of the body are in harmony, each with the other, we sense a feeling of bodily ease. When one or more of the organs of the body are under-stimulated or overtaxed, we feel states of pain or discomfort or a general feeling of uneasiness, or we feel tired, "run down," depressed, hungry, thirsty. The difficulty in the present world concerning the life sense is that this sense can become very confused. We can feel tired when we are not if we spend all of our time in "brain work"; we can feel hungry or thirsty when we are not, due to being stimulated by advertising, or becoming accustomed to food inundated with sugar; or we can be constantly nervous, which can be confused with being thirsty or hungry all the time; so can being bored. Disruption of the life sense results in the symptom of a vague sense of fear. This is because the sympathetic and parasympathetic nervous system is the pathway through which the life sense is experienced.

With this vague sense of fear comes the impulse to fix what is wrong. But what is wrong is not evident if there is no somatic illness. The disruption of bodily ease leads us to seek anything at all to quickly medicate the discomfort. We are led more and more to believe that somewhere there is a magic substance that will cure our dis-ease. We live in a mentality of addictive behavior toward what brings bodily ease, always willing to consume whatever will assuage the discomfort of the body, even if the pain is not specific.

Imbalances in the Life Sense

The life sense is perhaps under the most significant attack of all of the corporeal senses, as it is the sense in which we are most unconscious. As balance is experienced when we are comfortable in our bodies, the life sense is experienced when we are most uncomfortable in our bodies. When the inner organs come into some imbalance or are attacked by some outer organism, when we feel ill or succumb to a virus, or stump our toe in the dark, we are aware of our body in a different way and seek assistance to recover the ability to live in our body unconsciously. Pain gives us an acute presence of our body and makes us attend to it. When we are in pain, we are conscious of the life sense.

But now we see that the life sense can show us at least part of the reason disruptions in society are so prevalent. When discomfort and annoying symptoms arise, we react in absolute horror at the

17

idea of being indisposed, missing work or school, feeling bad for more than a few hours. Addictive behavior is, in part, the consequence of the cultural expectation of immediate alleviation of any uncomfortable consciousness of the body. (Equally, of course, addictive behavior stems from feeling totally excluded – from parents, home, work, economic life, and trauma.) In addition to the aversion of unpleasant physical sensations of the body, we are now experiencing an unwillingness to be present to and presented with the intrusions of emotional and psychological discomforts. Both physical and psychological pain can be a enormously important teacher, guiding us toward significant life changes. When the life sense is manipulated, controlled and tyrannized by forms of medicine and therapy that too easily and quickly dull the pain out of existence, we live in a social reality that promotes addictions of all sorts, and the propensity to senseless and unconscious violence.

There are other areas in which the life sense is disrupted. In our time, the clock dictates life, and we are socially conditioned to respond according to

18

the dictate of the hour of the day. But, as we once were more governed by a schedule, we are now becoming more and more governed by computer software. When we conform to a scheduled life, we leave natural time, enter the tempo of the clock and live at a pace mechanically derived from the fragmentation of clock time. Natural time eludes us now, although we fantasize about returning to its comforting flow.

The life sense can be restored by times of play and picnics, love and reunion, work and sleep, bath and stories. Such times have been supplanted by deadlines and meetings, workouts and working lunches, overwork and the dash for the commute. Now we enter the even more futile and crazed tempo of email and cell phones, fast food and faster faxes, multiple instantaneous meetings and mergers. We move at computer time, and as such are always thrown off balance by the instantaneousness with which everything can happen, with little touching us.

The space in which life occurs is the time of duration. Duration, once so integral a part of our sense of living, is now cut off from what we think to be "life." Life as duration offers itself to be touched and relished. Duration has been lost for the sake of the tempo in which we think we are supposed to exist but know to be hollow.

The life sense also makes it possible to develop the capacity of compassion. Knowing when one is well or ill involves more than knowing about one's own body. Illness teaches compassion for the other, but if discomfort has always been numbed, the necessary ground for feeling the suffering of others will be absent. Valuing the experience of illness does not preclude recovery from it, but it does allow that the illness itself has more to offer than the personal discomfort accompanying the disease. More evolves from it than the negative reaction of being sick. The disruption of the life sense, experienced as the need to diminish all pain, gives rise to 'victim consciousness', and 'entitlement', rather than developing capacities of being the comforter of others.

The "sense of balance", centered in the inner ear, senses the relationship between earth's gravity and our own body. When the sense of balance functions in a healthy way we are not only able to stand straight and upright, but we are also able to move around in the world without it 'swaying' or our becoming dizzy. Such a state of balance indicates we have a point of reference concerning the world and ourselves. There is also a subtler feeling; we feel inner calm and security. With the sense of balance, we take our place in the world as human beings between the sky above and the earth below, what is before us and behind us, and what is to either side of us.

In the present world, much throws us off balance. Vertigo is an extreme instance; for example, when there is an inner ear infection. But more subtle states of dizziness occur. When balance is not quite perfected, not fine tuned, so to say, vertigo feels more like a vague sense of being about to be swallowed up by the surrounding world. It is as if the ground could at any minute open, and we could fall in. In the modern world, we move from one activity to another throughout the day - answering the phone, taking care of children, going from one meeting to the next, trying to answer all the demands that come at us. Children in school have similar pressures; doing all the exercises, making sure they know what the teacher expects, keeping up with their friends and classmates, looking ok – did they bring their lunch or money, are they ready for after school activities, will they have a ride, is it safe to wait for the bus, or walk down the hall? After a few hours, we feel dizzy, disoriented. Adults can take a break, walk outside or go for a stretch, so that the sense of balance has a chance to recover. A child in school has no respite, and life is often lived out of balance, with no awareness of the source of the discomfort.

Disruptions of the Sense of Balance

In children, the sense of balance is assumed to be in place once they stand up. When a child reaches this milestone, he/she will begin to speak, and within a year or so start referring to himself or herself as "I." Standing upright is the fundamental gesture of the human being and the foundation for the capacity to refer to ourselves with this unique pronoun. Maintaining our equilibrium, our balance is the bodily gesture of the "I". When I stand up and feel dizzy or enter a room and am overwhelmed by the presence of someone I honor; or when I look out over the Grand Canyon, I can lose my equilibrium and become dizzy. Also, driving over a small but steep hill too quickly, running in circles as part of a game, or riding an amusement park ride can cause me to lose my equilibrium for a moment. I return to my inner sense of balance when I regain my focus and connect with a focal point in my immediate surrounding (through vision) or fill the space around me, whether it is the Grand Canyon or the night sky, with my own presence in it. When I do this, I am no longer dizzy, and have experienced the world holding me up, so to speak, by giving me my-self back.

But what if we never are sure of a point of reference due to a disruption of the sense of balance? And what would cause such a disturbance? The activity of the infant is the practice and rehearsal for the development of a sense of balance, and the ability to say "I," in the world. When the sense of balance is disturbed, the capacity we speak of as "I" always feels under attack. And because the sense of balance allows us to move from here to there, and still be ourselves, it is the origin for a certain quality of feeling sometimes referred to as a sense of freedom. When the "I" is always a little uncertain, a little undermined, we never experience the possibility of freedom. Freedom here is not political, but more the quality of being myself in the midst of millions of other selves and freely being able to mingle in and amongst them without losing my balance, and maybe becoming someone else.

Disruption of balance often results in very subtle feeling states. For example, for the young child who never quite has that comfortable feeling of filling the room, or of being given himself back by his environment, there is always a subtle, often indescribable discomfort, perhaps expressed as itchiness or inability to keep the room from wavering. Such children are always trying to compensate for what they experience as an unstable environment, so they move around. A lot. And if the room does not keep still, abstract symbols and pictures on papers do not stay still either, and in fact may add to the nauseous feeling by wavering counter to the room. Moving becomes an inner compulsion to stay in some relationship to the outer turmoil, and so they move to keep from being overwhelmed by the world. This is also referred to as attention deficit disorder. It is considered an epidemic in our schools. It is the response of the "I" under attack by the modern world, and we respond to the cry by diagnosis, medication, and behavior modification. The capacity to concentrate diminishes until destroyed and replaced with passive compliance to external regimentation and indoctrination. Balance and the sense of the free, human "I" are undermined.

But that is not all. The sense of balance is the basis for our capacity to trust. When we can stand firmly in and for ourselves and move into the world without the loss of our self, we develop an inner assurance about the world that participates with us in maintaining our own equilibrium; we develop

trust. With the I under attack, and the sense of
balance so often in jeopardy, there is very little trust
emerging from the realms of the educational
experience. If the world is never to be trusted we
perpetuate the frenzy to stay ahead of the dizzying
world and are denied the possibility to find a still
point for reflection, contemplation, rest, restoring
inner balance. The disruption of the sense of
balance unseats the trust we once had in our
capacity to meet the world and not be lost in it, in
our understanding of our selves in relation to others
in the world.

The "sense of movement" senses whether we are
still or in movement. We feel the movements of our
body primarily by means of the muscle system. This
system senses not only the larger movements of our
body, such as that of our arms and legs, or the
feeling of our neck when we move our head, but
also much more subtle movements, such as the
movement of the eyes, the movement of the fingers
and toes, the movement of our chest and belly when
we breath in and out. When the sense of movement
functions properly we experience a bodily sense of

26

being free. This feeling is quite remarkable. We get a feeling for this quality when we step outside in the sunshine and stretch or feel like we would like to run in the wind. In the present world, the sense of movement is either too cramped or it becomes too muscle bound.

Movement as a sense is quite amazing. It not only tells me I am choosing to move from here to there but also that the world is moving around me and in relationship to me. In young children and especially infants, movement is choreographed in relation to the sounds in the environment. Research has shown that the normal newborn moves in coordination with the sounds of the mother's voice. The activity of movement is even subtler than just the voluntary muscles in response to stimuli. Our eyes move with the things around us and inform our body on how to proceed. Our larynx moves in response to the voice of the other, and our muscles move in relation to the object. For example, to open the door, my body must have a "plan" to get to the door and turn the doorknob, before I set out to do so; otherwise I might not arrive at the door. This little plan is not

27

just about me but is in cooperation with the door. The door draws me to it, directs my movement as it were, to it. The plan completes when I open the door. Our sense of movement gives an inner feeling of purpose, of destiny. The sense of purpose fulfilled by the most insignificant of our movements is also present in the overriding gesture of life itself, as if we know where we are going and how to go about getting there. This phenomenon occurs when we encounter something and feel, "yes, I know this", or "I know I've met this person before"

Imbalances in the Sense of Movement

Sitting all day long, being carried from place to place in a car or a bus makes us feel cramped, not only in our muscles but also in our life. We also ask this of children from daycare through college, that they sit quietly and engage in an abnormal lack of activity, and engagement with information that does not move them inwardly. We replace the inner movement of imagination and wonder with empty entertainment and stimulation to "hold" their attention. The inner sense of movement dims, and we feel more like we are lugging our body around. On the other hand, the ways in which we try to balance the feeling of being cramped through going to the gym and working out on the exercise machines, jogging, playing games such as football or basketball, do not result in a healthy sense of movement either. We may feel a tingling in our muscles and get a temporary high from the increase in blood circulation, but it is more like a momentary breaking through the barrier of confinement, which does not, however, give us the ongoing corporeal feeling of freedom. For children, the disruption of this sense is most dramatic and often leads to a serious misunderstanding of the behavior of the child. Psychological reasons are sought out for hyperactivity and a host of other "learning difficulties", while the basis for such disorders goes unrecognized.

The nature of movement that must participate with a plan to fulfill the purpose, needs careful attention in education. To read or write, spell or do math problems require a certain quality of movement. Should one's sense of movement be disrupted in subtle ways, what must the all important school task of reading, or writing become? When we learn to read, the letters must each be looked at individually, usually speaking their sound out loud one at a time. Slowly we begin to put sounds together and meet the next letter with recognition. Soon we skim through the letter part and experience the whole word, and then the whole of the sentence, in the activity of reading. This task takes place through movement across and down the page. These are extremely fine tuned movements. Disruption of the sense of movement brings subtle demands on the sense itself. We call this attack and disruption of the of movement dyslexia. We treat this disruption by remediation, as if the person were slow witted, and never recognize the qualities of the sense of movement that can not be expressed.

The sense of movement makes possible the capacity for an inner sense of purpose, instilling an assurance that there is a reason for existence and I am here for a unique reason. Knowing I have a purpose is the bodily basis for a capacity for faith. It gives life rhythm and direction. But the sense of movement is disrupted by our very ability to learn by imitation and move in relation to the world we are born into. For example, if all we hear all day from birth are the mechanical, electronic sounds of television and stereo, this will inflict a certain character on the way we move. In addition, if we are shuttled about in cars, buses, subways, carried, pushed and hauled in and out of mechanical conveyances, taken to malls, grocery stores and downtown where people are rushing and hurrying about, much like automobiles driving on the highway, our initial experience of movement is something mechanical, which we imitate with the first forays we take into being part of the world. We move like machines.

Today even children learn to move with the instantaneousness of the computer and will be at even more of a disadvantage with the movement of the written word, for this new technology will most likely bring about more profound disruption to the sense of movement. Watch for an increase in individuals with dyslexia of all kinds.

The sense of touch. The whole of the body is the organ for the "sense of touch". When the sense of

touch functions in a healthy way, in our contact
with the surrounding world we feel an instinctual
sense of divine quality, as being a part of everything
that surrounds us. The sense of touch gives us a
feeling of the interior liveliness of our own body.
To the sense of touch, the outer world is not given
to us in a way that we can know the particularities
of each thing we touch. When we touch something
or are touched by something or someone, we come
up against resistance. What the outer thing is cannot
be known by touch alone - vision, movement, and
other senses are needed for this; we come up against
the world as something other than our body; that
feels very mysterious like we have come up against
a very great mystery. If we are not touched, the
liveliness of our own body is dimmed. When,
however, we touch or are touched by too many
artificial things like plastic, hard, sharp or angular
things, the world as manufactured and artificial
instead of being experienced as a divine mystery,
the world instills us with fear.

Imbalances in the Sense of Touch

If touch introduces us to the mystery of the other and gives us back a reflection that is a sense for the mystery within the unknown border of our selves, touch is also the origin from a bodily perspective, for any feeling we have for the mystery of what is not us, what is perhaps called spiritual, or even divine. Touch allows us to develop capacities for a sense of boundaries but also introduces us to the border as worlds of possibilities for discovery. Boundaries in and of themselves offer a moral signature, a place that one crosses with care and respect. The disruption of the sense of touch creates the breakdown of the capacity to experience the other as a mystery. The other becomes merely object, perhaps plastic or paper, utilitarian, able to be used to fulfill my impulses, drives or desires. Possibilities for violence against others magnify, or withdrawal from others becomes necessary to create safety for my own personal boundary. The phenomenon of autism comes to mind.

Disruption of the sense of touch is rampant in our society. We have lost a sense for the divine, and therefore for the mystery and wonder which is not us. What is not us has become a manufactured object, available for our manipulation, destruction or adoration and collection.

The relation of soul to the sense of touch, and indeed, to all the corporeal senses is one in which the inner life of soul works from within the body outward toward the surrounding world. The lower senses form a border area between soul and body. This border area is experienced as impulses and drives when viewed from the bodily side of this border. When viewed from the soul side of this border, it is desire that is experienced. Impulses, drives, and desires then constitute the soul of the corporeal senses and prepare us for action in the world.

When the corporeal senses are disrupted, disturbed, disordered, when they encounter the surrounding world that is manipulated to a high degree, we become unable to move out into the world in harmonious ways that meet with and joins the world so that our actions cooperate with the surrounding world, add to its wholeness. Instead, what happens

34

is that when our sense experiences are derived more from manipulations of the outer world than immediate experiences of the surrounding world, then impulses, drives and desires are typically stronger than they otherwise would be. We thus become less and less able to contain our impulses, drives and desires where they can deepen the inner qualities of life. Inwardly we are too stirred up, and so act in impulsive ways, are driven to do things that are not beneficial for either our health or well being. We feel a terrible need to satisfy our desires immediately.

The Middle, or World Senses: Descriptions, Imbalances and Healing

The Four Middle, or World Senses

While the corporeal senses are the basis of will, the middle, or world senses are the basis of the feeling life. The term "world" is used because this middle grouping of senses has to do with the communion of the body with the world. These senses are smell, vision, taste and the warmth sense. When these senses are dulled or disrupted, the overall result is a dulling in the feeling realm for the world. We then become tremendously interested in feelings but take them to be entirely our inner states. We try to make ourselves feel by all sorts of psychological therapies, or stimulants of all kinds, not realizing that the fundamental problem lies in the fact that we have lost the intimate relationship with the outer world.

The word "feeling" means "touch". "Touch" has a dual direction. On the one hand, feeling means to touch inwardly. Feeling is to be touched inwardly by the world. But, feeling as "touch" also implies a movement outward; our soul, or feeling life, moves outward into the world to make a connection with it. The four world senses all have this characteristic, each in different ways, of drawing the world into ourselves and going out to meet the world through the soul.

With the sense of smell, the exchange between our physical being and the world occurs through the element of air. Odors work through the air element to bring the world into our body. There are some specific aspects of feeling life related to this sense and the gesture of bringing the world into the body. We cannot open and close our nose as we do our eyes or our mouth; through smell, we remain open and vulnerable to the world. One of the most uncomfortable aspects of having a cold is not being able to smell. Smell gives us the most intimate feeling of the world.

The world surrounding the body comes into the interior of the body and is met by the soul, where we have an experience of the substance of the world in an intimate way. We experience many different odors. There is a tendency to lose ourselves in smell; smell permeates us. If you smell a rose, it is experienced everywhere in the body. The smell takes over, and it takes a while to recover from the moment of becoming a rose. Unlike the animals, who live in and are part of the world of smells all of the time as instinctual, we have more distance and are not in smell all of the time; that is, it does not overcome our consciousness except when the odor is powerful. Even then, after a while, we recover our consciousness and discrimination from the smell.

Smell brings a particular feeling quality of the world. Picture smelling a rose, then picture smelling a rotten egg. The first smells good and the second smells bad. We might be able to find a more refined language to express the difference, but it would still have these two qualities. It is quite amazing that qualities of smell are felt in this way, that the substance of the world reveals itself in these two ways. To speak of something smelling good and another thing smelling bad is not an intellectual judgment, nor a conclusion that we arrive at. They are the immediately given qualities of the world. We experience smell as a moral quality. The most basic feeling we have is moral feeling. Smell gives us the bodily basis for moral judgment; while it is not in itself moral judgment. Caustic soap smells bad, but it may be very good for certain things.

But what happens when odor becomes manipulated? For example, the smell of lavender may permeate caustic soap. Right at the level of the body, we are introduced to cover ups. Right at the level of the body we are given a kind of life instruction that says we can make things appear however we want them to appear. Perhaps the capacity of lying is instilled long before we know anything about moral choices.

Care for the sense of smell has to do with becoming conscious that in our time, the sense of smell is inherently experienced metaphorically. Caustic soap saturated with the odor of lavender smells **like** lavender. A lavender flower smells lavender, not **like** lavender. The only way to avoid being taken into a world full of lies is the development of "metaphor awareness." An orange smells orange. Shampoo made to smell orange smells **like** an orange. Things really cannot be made to smell other than they are; they can only be made to smell **as if** they were something other than they are. The metaphorical capacity is very interesting. The rational intellect cannot think metaphorically. 'A' cannot at the same time be 'B' for the intellect. But imagination can and does combine things that do not rationally belong together. Healing the disordered smell world has to do with the development of the capacity of imagination. If caustic soap smells **like** lavender, that also means it also does not smell like lavender. The caustic smell cannot be completely covered, and if it is, the odor of lavender is so strong that no lavender ever smelled that particular way.

For children, smell can be especially confusing. We place expectations on young children by our assumption that smell functions automatically, and that very little ever needs to be addressed in the education of smells. Besides, by only treating smell as one of the "five" senses, we assume there is not a connection between what we smell and how our feelings evolve. Education should not be taken as literal in the realm of the senses but should approach the child in the realm of imagination. We expect children to have wonderful imaginative capacities, but what do we do to the very foundation of imagination by the physical disruption and dishonesty of the sense of smell? In everything from crayons to pictures in books, to the food we eat, we deceive and disguise, lie and steal the real smell of the world, and replace it with deception.

Taste could well be called the cultural sense. How we make things in the world depends a great deal on taste. It is not by accident that the word 'taste' refers to the experience of flavors in the mouth, and also to a primary characteristic of constituting culture. But the most essential quality of taste, having a sense of taste, the one that defines the value of taste in the bodily realm, is almost completely lost. Thus,

41

we are tremendously confused about what constitutes culture. We certainly have great diversity in the sense taste, and diversity is also important to culture. However, there is something even more important. When we taste something, regardless of the particular flavor, we have the capacity of tasting whether what we are eating is wholesome or unwholesome, healthy or unhealthy. This is an actual quality of taste, but it is nearly completely lost as a tasting capacity. Thus, the question of whether what we make in the world is healthy, not only for us, but for others and for the rest of the earth, is either not considered or is confused.

The word "taste" comes from Middle English *tasten*, which means to examine, to test, to sample. Taste is a transition zone between our body and the world. We are sampling or testing the world to find out what it is like in all its variety. However, we are also being sampled by the world as it turns itself into us. Just imagine all of the things people eat. The earth offers about 20,000 edible plants alone. And besides the foods we are accustomed to in our culture, other cultures value tastes such as that of rodents, grasshoppers, snakes, kangaroos, snails, bats, turtles or piranha.

We are most sensitive to bitter tastes. The taste buds can detect bitterness if it exists in the ratio of one part in 2,000,000. We can detect something sour in the ratio of one part in 130,000; something salty, one part in 400; and something sweet one part in 200. Different parts of the tongue detect these tastes; sweet things at the tip of the tongue; bitter things at the back of the tongue; sour things at the sides; salty taste spread over the surface, but mainly up front. There are revealing metaphors here. Salty taste enhances any taste, as it is all over the surface. The taste of salt is also right up front, easily recognizable. Bitterness runs deep. Sweet is the first introduction; sour comes at you from the side. Since bitter and sour are the most sensitive aspects of taste, it would seem that these aspects of the world are what we are really meant to come to terms with. It is most interesting then, that we cover them over, mainly by adding sugar to practically everything. Salt also becomes a covering once it goes beyond the limit of enhancing. Thus, we get a picture that in the present world the sensitivity of taste has been reversed. We imagine the world as if it should be all sweetness; but, once the body has taken in so much sweet flavor, that is the way the body approaches the world - not being sweet but expecting everything to be sweet. On the other hand, we can imagine that if we were more in touch with bitterness and sourness, the quality of sweetness in something, we would come to realize, has to be developed out of our own inner soul forces.

Taste is more active than the sense of smell. We are always open to smell. We have to open our mouth to taste. And we have to be active to taste - chewing, dissolving, swallowing. Also, we have to add something to the world of taste saliva. More will be involved in tasting. We actively engage the substance of the world. Sweetening works against the will element of engaging the world. Sugar is ego food; it strokes us, makes us feel good and with sweets, there is a tendency to take them in, and then want more and more. Bitterness, on the other hand, develops the will. Sour awakens the will, and salt keeps taste alert, it brings taste to consciousness.

With smell, we become the world. When I smell a rose, I become rose. With taste, there is a two way conversation. We become what we taste, and it becomes us. Taste is the transition moment of this exchange. What we taste is the instant of transition. We take a piece of the world in, and this becomes the substance of our body.

Taste has now become part of the world of virtual reality. Artificial flavors were invented in the early 19th century, but it was not until the 1960's that they became prevalent. The cultural history of tastes probably follows much the same pattern as that of odors. Virtually the whole spectrum of food flavors has been artificially constructed. The majority of food on the supermarket shelf has some form of artificial flavor. Sugar dominates. It is now possible to create a virtual chicken. Manufacturers can mold a chicken shape from vegetable protein and then add imitation chicken breast flavor, chicken fat flavor, chicken skin flavor, and basic chicken flavor. These are all chemical flavorings, known as "flavoromatics". This virtual chicken would, of course, taste <u>like</u> chicken. Hundreds of flavors are involved with chicken. Only a few of these are artificially developed, but these are heightened while the other, more subtle flavors are allowed to drop away. It would seem that the soul effect of simplifying taste in such a manner would be that we would also lose the capacity to face the subtle and complex aspects of life. Again, it is the metaphorical, imaginative capacity that needs to be developed in order not to be taken over by virtual food, and in its wake, virtual values of every sort that define our culture.

The concept of "family values", "ethical values", "economic values", political "values" of all sorts are the cultural abstraction of the sense of taste. As such, education of "values" can be theoretically applied to educational curriculum, with no sense of the true nature of the value ever being conveyed.

The sense of vision, sight, is a primary sense through which we feel. The blind person

notwithstanding, the predominate, tyrannical sense
through which we relate to the world is vision. We
usually only look at one perspective of vision. This
view says that the eye the organ of sight is merely
an extension of the brain connecting to the surface
of the face. When the optometrist looks into our
eyes, he is looking directly at the brain. The
corporeal senses are all transformations of the skin,
and through them we commune with the flesh of the
world. But the eye, tends to have an intellectual
view of the world.

There are more mysteries to vision than the
tendency to see the world intellectually. The eye is
colored. Not only are there blue and brown and
green eyes, but every iris, no matter what the
dominating color, also contains a range of other
colors as well. Then there is another quality of
vision related to color. When we look at one color
for a time and then close our eyes, we see the
opposite color something that occurs only with the
sense of vision. When we taste something bitter, the
opposite, sweet, does not complement it. The
miracle of sight is that the eye complements what is

missing. The soul is quite close to the surface with vision because the complimentary color we experience is the activity of the soul completing what is missing.

Vision apprehends only two things - shapes and colors. The apprehension of shape is closely related to the eye brain connection, but the apprehension of color is not an intellectual experience, but an emotional one. With color, the basic quality of mood of soul is expressed in relation with the world. Further, color in the world expresses something of the inner qualities of things in the world. The colors of fall leaves do not just create a mood in us; they are a mood of the world, its inner, soul quality at the time of Autumn. The mood of the world is quite different in the Summer, with all of the green, quite different in Spring with the blossoming of all kinds of colors and different still in Winter, when things turn toward being gray and white. The soul of the world actually goes into the interior of the earth during the Winter. With color, nature displays her inner workings to the outer world.

Color is another bodily basis for feeling. One can then wonder what happens to feeling when one works eight or more hours a day in an office building in which the predominant shade is white, (which is not a color). What happens when the cinema comes along, technicolor introduced, with color TV, magazine graphics and smartphone snapshots? These amazing inventions, which is not at all like the color we encounter in the world, but more like paint that has been splashed over the scenery, reveal only surfaces. Behind these imaged surfaces there is no soul, no life of feeling and relationship, no possibility of reflection and contemplation; but only decoration, stimulation, and expectation of reaction. On the surface, the color is too vivid, too colored, too correctly simulated, rather than the play of light and shadow creating color. The colors are used for effect, hitting you over the head with emotion, vs. creating a mood, setting a backdrop, inviting one to participate. Too much exposure to this type of thing and we begin to experience the world as painted rather than as full of colors that are every moment coming into being, changing, disappearing, reappearing. Colors play. Paint covers. When I look out my window every evening at sunset, the purple and red and orange and blue and gray of the sky changes from one second to the next; it is a beautiful experience of how color is every moment creating. There is an unmistakable spiritual dimension to the world of color, which gets lost with surfaces that look painted.

The difference between color expressing the inner, soul qualities of the world, and artificial color has yet another dimension. We look at colored surfaces. We become involved in the world of color. What this means is that we become involved in the world as color because the eye is the sense organ that actually contains all the other sense capacities. Vision encompasses all of the other senses. That is why we can speak of all of the other senses through metaphors that are basically visual. We cannot speak of the eye by means of smell, but we can talk about smell by means of vision. If I say that odor comes into the nose, carried by the air, you will notice that you have a visual picture of this process. The visual system is connected with most of the

other senses. For example, the capacity of balance
also works through the eye. We partly keep our
balance through the eye. There are four muscles for
moving the eye, up and down, right and left, plus
muscles that make possible for a rotary movement
of the eye. These play into the sense of balance, and
also very much into the sense of movement. We
also see sweet colors, dirty colors, as well as warm
and cool colors. The eye is the all encompassing
sense organ, and as such is often the tyrannical
source of overcompensation of the disruptions in
other, more subtle senses, such as balance and
movement.

The care for the sense of vision has to do with
learning to pay attention to the play of color,
primarily in the natural world. As children live more
and more in simulated environments, the focus on
the natural world tends to become dramatically
decreased. (This statement is somewhat relative,
i.e., if you live on the plains of Wyoming vs. the
suburbs or any city, the child's experience of the
world as given is different; but the value of the
simulated object vs. the natural world may remain

the same, canceling out the quality of the difference.) Thus, seeing, vision, as a sense is not just whether it functions adequately or not, a matter of periodic checkups, but the act of seeing and thus of feeling can be enhanced, manipulated, repressed or entirely distorted. We must learn to look with its attendant moods, and as such, sensitive seeing can be taught. A curriculum for seeing is rather like religious education, and therefore must be taken on with great care and concern for values and conscience.

The warmth sense. In this grouping of the senses through which the body comes into communion with the world, there is one final sense that gets very little attention. Science is aware of this sense but has done little to investigate it, and when it has, the results are varied and unclear. This sense is the sense of warmth and cold or the temperature sense. We sense the difference between the warmth of our body and the warmth or coldness of things outside our body. This sensing has nothing to do with absolute temperature. For example, a common experiment is to take three bowls of water. Fill one

with ice water, one with hot water, and one with
lukewarm water. Put your left hand into the bowl of
ice water for five minutes, and at the same time, put
your right hand into the hot water for the same
amount of time. Then put both hands into the bowl
of lukewarm water. To the left hand, the water will
feel hot, and to the right, the water will feel cold.
The water, measured by a thermometer is a given
temperature, but we feel it differently with each
hand. This is a good way to get a sense of the
warmth sense. Something has to happen between
our body and the world for us to experience
temperature. There has to be a flow. When heat
flows from the body into the outer world, the
experience is one of coldness. The flow of warmth
away from the body is coldness. When we grasp a
hot object, heat flows from the object into us and we
feel warmth. This description is simple physics. But
the question remains, where does the experience
come from?

The flow of warmth away from the body is a
contraction of the soul. The soul reaches out to the
world, and when it receives nothing back, this is the

53

experience of coldness. The warmth sense is the bodily basis for a similar dimension in our relationships with others. When we reach out to someone and receive nothing back, there is also the experience of coldness, although here it is much more a pure soul experience. However, a person can leave you cold, and that coldness is felt in the body, almost like temperature. On the other hand, when we open ourselves up to the world and receive something back, we feel warmth; it is similar to our relationships with another person. From the viewpoint of the soul, the warmth sense has to do with our interest in the world. It has to do with that ongoing flow that is going on between ourselves and the world and between the world and us.

We see more and more reliance on technological equipment to stimulate and entertain children and therefore keep their attention. When "attention" is held be mere stimulation of nerve impulses, there develops a deep mistrust of feeling. Stimulation becomes necessary to feel warmth, or aliveness, at the expense of relationship and trust in other human beings. Computers, films, TV, etc., take the place of the warmth of human exchange and presence, and a capacity to give of oneself to another cannot develop. Also, when the temperature becomes evenly regulated, with air conditioning, or forced air heat, both of which are entirely a part of our culture, it becomes most likely that the capacity of interest in the world and even in others dulls. We may have an intellectual curiosity, but the body is more or less left out in the cold unless the heat of passion is involved. The warmth sense is even more essential than vision; in a way, it is the basis of all of the world senses, for if there is no interest in the world, the other three are already dulled.

Healing the Four World Senses

To summarize, the four senses called 'world' senses; with the sense of smell, the exchange between our bodily being and the world occurs through the element of air. Odors work through the air element to bring the world into our body. With the sense of taste, the exchange between our body and the world occurs in the element of water. A substance is brought into the mouth, where it is there dissolved in the fluid of saliva. In the case of vision, the exchange occurs between our soul and the soul of the world. Color, for example, is not just on the surface of things but expresses the inner qualities of the outer world the earth element. And in the sense of warmth, flow is required between our body and the world. Warmth or coldness relies on the flow of heat. The flow is related to the element of fire.

This alchemical imagination of the world senses shows their relationship to the world based on the four primary elements of Earth, Air, Fire, and Water. The reason for introducing such an alchemical image is to bring out that there is a creative process occurring in the sensing of the outer world. It is not just a matter of receiving impressions of an already fixed and completed world. For the world to be there, as experience, we have to be creatively involved with the world and it with us; sensing here is creation happening. The alchemists understood the responsibility of being involved in creating in this way through the senses. If the world senses are dulled, the ongoing creation in this way through the senses diminishes. Proper

56

care, even education of the world senses is to take up the responsibility of being involved in creation, not just using and consuming it for our purposes.

A few comments have been made concerning how to go about strengthening each of the four world senses. Part of the difficulty with these senses is that the sense organs for each of these senses is different. That means that it is possible for each of these senses to be dulled one by one in the conditions of the present world. There must be a way that these senses do not become rigidly separated, for if they do, the feeling life, even if it exists, undergoes dismemberment.

The care of the world senses can be best attended by means of the art of painting. Painting is not at all simply something visual. It is a way of working in a disciplined way in the realm of feeling, of keeping feeling whole. When one is working with red, blue, purple, yellow, any color, there is also a subtle sense of taste, a soul like quality that has to do with taste. So, with painting, vision and taste are brought into ongoing relation. Working artistically with color also brings vision into ongoing relation with the sense of warmth. When we say red is hot and blue is cool, there is a real basis for this in the color. And each stimulates smell in a subtle way, having nothing to do with the overt smell of the paint. Great care must be taken in painting, however, that also respects the age and experience of the child in school. For example, young children are better served by painting with light and watercolor paint, as opposed to the heavy and dense oil or even water based acrylics.

The emphasis here is that artistic work is not an arbitrary idea related to education but an absolute necessity. Artistic work is a necessity if the four middle senses are not to become too separated. Art is not a frivolous extra in school; it is crucial to form the basis for a healthy feeling life.

But it is not just adding art to the curriculum for children that is needed. Adults also need to begin to paint to bring balance and healing into their own sense life. For the adult, also spending time with good paintings, developing a real relationship with

58

them, can be healing for these four world senses. Here, it is important to stay away from interpreters of art, from historians of art, from critics of art, for most often these disciplines take us away from the immediate sense experience of art. They tend to teach us to look away, or to look at, rather than to become involved in the immediate sensed experience with art.

The Higher, or Communal Senses: Descriptions, Imbalances and Healing

The Four Higher, or Communal Senses

According to Rudolf Steiner, only one of the higher senses is recognized as a sense at all -- the sense of hearing. The other three higher senses are the word or speech sense, the thought sense, and the ego sense. The disorders of the sense life that we have spoken of could not be balanced only through the suggestions made. A new liveliness, spirit, vigor, interest in and for the senses can come about through learning to experience the communal or relational senses.

These senses too are being dulled, more so because they are not even recognized. Once they are, and paid attention to by adults, sensing in these realms goes a long way toward healing all the senses. The communal senses have to do with sensing qualities of other human beings. They could also be called the inter relational senses.

The first of these senses, hearing, is more of a transitional sense between the world senses and the communal senses. The language sense is the bodily capacity to sense the speaking of another person. The thought sense concerns the capacity to bodily perceive that another person is engaged in thinking, though it does not include directly perceiving the thought content. The sense of "I" or individuality involves developing the capacity to sense the particular quality of the other that is their own, unique individual being. Part of the work in considering these senses is to begin to observe and see if you can actually experience them.

Each of the communal senses correlates with one of the corporeal senses. The sense of touch correlates with the sense of the I; the life sense with the thought sense; balance with hearing; and movement with the speech sense. Because of the particular polarities between the corporeal and communal senses, healing and balancing of the corporeal senses can be approached through the development of the higher senses. However, this healing takes place through relationships.

When, even if but for a few moments, I can experience in a direct, bodily manner, something of the true individuality of another person, that sensing acts on the other as a kind of spiritual touch, and the person feels more at home with their body. When I attend to another person in such a manner as to sense their engagement in creative thinking, that can be healing to the life sense of the other person. When I truly listen to another person, such hearing also acts to bring alignment of balance; and when I pay intimate attention to the speech of another, that sensory attention also acts to bring the sense of movement of that person into equilibrium. Care of the communal senses is the responsibility of all adults who interact with children, especially in schools. It is the adult who must seek the development of these senses and bring them to bear on who they are as teachers and what they do in teaching.

Let us now consider each of the communal senses.

Hearing, as a higher sense, involves becoming conscious of the two sides of hearing - that it gives us the inner qualities of the outer world, and that it also gives us, through the body, an earthly experience of the spiritual nature of another person. Hearing a bell, a siren, the wind blowing through the trees is something quite different than hearing the voice of another person. Hearing the sounds of the world gives us a sense of the inner qualities of things, but hearing another person gives us an immediate sense of the inner soul life of the person. We hear fear, or desire, or need, or intimacy.

The sacred quality of hearing is disrupted by electronic intervention in the present world. Not only recording, amplification, digitalizing, but also the intervention of the telephone, where voice is separated from bodily presence and human gesture. As with all of the senses, none of these things are bad or wrong, or to be completely avoided. However, we must become conscious of what they do and always make sure that balance is provided --

real music, real conversation, real speaking, real hearing, real listening. Such balance also recognizes that the corporeal 'sense of balance' is affected by hearing,

The sense of speech, or language is also involved at this level in how the world is being currently created. The speech sense is not just knowing I or another is speaking, but the specific capacity to sense the word, even in an unknown foreign language, as human language. The language spoken may have a musical quality to it, but we recognize the words and must quiet the words in us to hear the words of another. The hearing of the spoken words of another is possible because we follow the movements of the others larynx with our own as they speak. We 'speak' with them. But this is an inner gesture, and our outer speaking must be silenced to hear the other. As such, to hear language we have to deliberately quiet ourselves and our movement to be present to the other's speech. Very often, when we do not put ourselves aside in this way, we really do not hear what another person is saying. Because we know words and their meaning,

64

we think we know what the person is saying, but we do not. We only hear what we already think.

Hearing language is a highly spiritual act. We have to hold our own personality in abeyance in order to hear another's speech. We have to sacrifice what we are feeling and thinking, our judgment, and become present to the language itself.

When I listen to someone speak, my larynx is also active. Therefore, listening is also always speaking, but it is speaking what the person speaking to me is speaking. We typically are not aware of this. Heard language crosses over into speaking language. This is a helpful image because it shows how intimate language really is. When language is conceived only as a means of communication, we have a theory of language that leaves us lonely. From the point of view of communication, language does not convey anything of the person, but only what the person communicates. But through understanding something of the language sense, we see that language is not communication, but communion.

Beyond hearing language and the sensory capacity to recognize the language, we have the sensory capacity to understand what is said through language. In order to understand meaning, language itself becomes transparent. The concepts we understand are not identical with the language we speak. Language passes on an idea, but never completely. When we have an idea, it is often terribly difficult to find just the right words to express it. When we do find the right words, they are never quite adequate. Not really having said what we meant, or not being able to express what we really meant to this particular person, or not being able to put into words what we are thinking, is an experience we have all had from time to time. The thought sense, considered further below, however, moves the other way. Through this sense, we perceive first that someone else is thinking, and immediately sense, usually through language, the meaning of what the person is thinking. In order to understand someone, language has to be erased. I do not pay attention to the words, but what is meant by the words. The ideas conveyed by language are silent.

The thought sense. Many people do not really originate ideas these days -- they rely on ideas that are like old coins circulating. Thus, it is not too surprising that the thought sense goes unrecognized. When we only use language that has been used, in the ways it has been used by others, we feel we are thinking when we are just passing on used, already thought ideas. When children are taught already thought ideas to the exclusion of how to think, when information takes precedence over thinking, the thought sense becomes dulled.

A great deal of sacrifice is necessary to create an idea, to come up with concepts. It is difficult even to take ideas and express them anew out of ourselves, so that they become essentially new ideas. Why there is such a paucity of ideas is that thinking anew requires holding back what I may be feeling not denying it, but not letting it interfere with the act of thinking. All of the senses we have thus far considered have to be present but held back in the act of thinking. And, if the senses are disordered, then we are too occupied with those

67

senses to be able to hold them back. When we think, which is different than using ideas as information, we have to put aside our feelings, emotions, desires, self concerns, even life concerns in order to make the inner space where ideas can come and dwell.

The thought sense does not directly concern the capacity of thinking, but it is certainly involved. The thought sense perceives the thinking of another person; through this sense we are able to understand another person. In order to perceive the thought of another, a particular kind of attention is involved. To be an attentive listener, I must develop the capacity of hearing, of language and of having true ideas, not simply taking up those used by others. If I have not developed these capacities, I cannot truly understand the other person. I also cannot understand the other person if I am occupied with my own ideas. I have to have the capacity, at the moment of listening, to extinguish my own thinking and put the thinking of the other person in its place. The thought sense requires selflessness.

There are two main disorders of the thought sense. The first is that it may not develop, particularly in a world in which we mistake information to be thought. To develop this sense, and as well the other communal senses, the individual must be willing to remain child like until the end of life. The best teachers we always remember were not the ones who were trying to teach us something, which is nothing more than indoctrination. The best teachers were those who were willing to stand up in front of the class and think. Observing this happen was the greatest inspiration. What joy to observe wonder, curiosity, interest, experimentation, openness all very child like qualities.

The second disorder lies in the tendency to develop the capacity of thinking in egotistical ways. Thinking, when it is valued at all, tends to be promoted only for what it can do for us. It may mean we can enjoy the act of thinking, read important books, it makes possible entering a professional field. Almost never is it considered to be the necessary preparation for being able to be selflessly present to others.

The sense of individuality, the "I" sense, does not
refer to experiencing ourselves as individuals but to
experiencing another person as an individual.
Sensing the individuality of another person is a
spiritual act, occurring through the body. The sense
organ for sensing individuality is the whole of the
human body and is actually most related to touch.
The mark of sensing individuality is most often
strife, much more so than harmonious acceptance.
When I perceive something of the individuality of
another, there is likely to be a struggle. As long as I
hear what I like or want to hear, nothing within me
is challenged and nothing truly new comes through.
To become aware of this sense requires meeting
one's own fears of being challenged, of not
knowing, of being permeated with the mysterious
nature of another person.

We have to understand that we are afraid of the
unknown, whether it be in others or ourselves. This
fear is quite healthy, for it prompts the development
of spiritual courage. Of course, strife can be purely
a clash of egotism with egotism. However, the

experience of strife is quite different than a battle of egos. It is to perceive another as completely other, not like me nor anyone I know. This can be a painful experience, perhaps one in which we feel diminished, but also a moment of enormous respect. A feeling of the sacred center of the being of the other person develops. For this reason, the sense of individuality is quite confused in our time. It is a sense that is in the process of developing, and quickly goes unnoticed.

Every form of mass movement works against this sense working correctly. A tremendously powerful leveling process operates in our culture; everyone is supposed to be like everyone else. The whole of our current educational system is based, however innocuously conceived, on this premise. It is the basis for the indoctrination that we all receive, whether in public or private school, to become a member of this society. In addition, the people who are outstanding (meaning simply that they stand out, not that they are somehow 'greater') - politicians, entertainers, sports heroes present us with images, or packages, of themselves, not with their actual self.

This sense is very difficult to care for in our self-indulgent culture. With the disruptions of the corporeal senses, in particular, those who have experienced harm through abuse, an understandable need to feel the self in a bodily way emerges. But this diminishes the capacity to truly experience the other, because we have so little of ourselves, and there for little capacity for self sacrifice. The care and development of this sense require awakening to a sense of true service, which in itself involves purification of the soul.

Care of three of the communal senses - the language sense, the thought sense, and the sense of individuality require a special sort of attention because these three communal, or inter relational senses are not yet completely developed in our time; they are still in the process of becoming an integral part of our being in humanity as a whole, and they develop in the individual throughout life. The greatest hindrance to their developing throughout life is brought about by disturbances in the corporeal senses, which occur very early in life. If the corporeal senses are disordered, the relational senses cannot develop. The sense organs for the corporeal senses are the body as a whole, even though sensing may take particular bodily pathways. The sense organs for relational senses are also the whole body. There is an intimate connection between these higher senses and the middle and lower ones.

The movement, balance, touch and life sense are all integral to the early years of education, and as such, could be profoundly nurtured in the formative, first years of school, when the will of the individual is most in need of developing with inner strength. The senses of smell, taste, vision lower and warmth, the middle senses, as the foundation for the life of feeling, could be addressed through the imagination and development of true artistic capacity in the middle years of education, giving the world individuals with conscience and true depth of feeling for the earth and all who live here. From this solid basis the capacity for true, living thinking

could develop, blossoming from the unfolding of
the senses of hearing, the speech, thought and "I"
sense, creating a true culture, a world, unimaginable
to the technical imagination bent on making us all
efficient processing devices.

Cheryl Sanders Sardello, &Robert Sardello,

References
Relevant Works on the Senses

Abram, D. 1996. *The Spell of the Sensuous*. New York: Pantheon Books.

Ackerman, D. 1990. *A Natural History of the Senses*. New York: Random House.

Aeppli, W. n.d. *The Care and Development of the Human Senses*. Forest Row: Steiner Schools Fellowship in Great Britain.

Konig, K. 1960. *The Circle of the Twelve Senses*. Lecture given at the Waldorf Institute, Spring Valley, N.Y.

Konig, K. 1984. *The First Three Years of the Child*. Hudson, N.Y.: Anthroposophic Press.

Soesman, A. *The Twelve Senses*, Trans. Jacob Cornelis. Glos., U.K: Hawthorn Press. (distributed by Anthroposophic Press, Hudson, N.Y.)

Steiner, R. 1996. *Anthroposophy A Fragment*. Hudson, N.Y.: Anthroposophic Press.

Relevant Works in Existential Phenomenology

Levin, D. M. 1985. *The Body's Recollection of Being.* London: Routledge & Kegan Paul.

Merleau Ponty, M. 1962. *Phenomenology of Perception.* London: Routledge & Kegan Paul.

Merleau Ponty, M. 1964. *The Primacy of Perception.* Evanston: Northwestern University Press.

van den Berg, J. 1972. *A Different Existence: Principles of Phenomenological Psychology.* Pittsburgh: Duquesne University Press.

Relevant Works in Jungian Psychology

Hillman, J. 1979. *Re Visioning Psychology.* New York: Harper & Row.

Jung, C. 1964. *Civilization in Transition.* Collected Works, Vol. 10 Princeton: Princeton University Press.

Jung, C. 1968. *The Structure and Dynamics of the Psyche.* Collected Works, Vol. 8. Princeton: Princeton University Press.

Sardello, R. 1992. *Facing the World with Soul.* New York: HarperCollins.

Sardello, R. 1995. *Love and the Soul: Creating a Future for Earth*. New York: HarperCollins.

Relevant Works of Rudolf Steiner

Steiner, R. 1981. *A Modern Art of Education*. London: Rudolf Steiner Press.

Steiner, R. 1974. *The Kingdom of Childhood*. London: Rudolf Steiner Press.

Steiner, R. 1982. *Colour*. London: Rudolf Steiner Press.

Steiner, R. 1966. *Study of Man*. London: Rudolf Steiner Press.

Steiner, R. 1972. *Curative Education*. London: Rudolf Steiner Press.

Steiner, R. 1983. *Deeper Insights into Education*. Hudson N.Y.: Anthroposophic Press.

Steiner, R. 1988. The Child's Changing Consciousness and Waldorf Education. Hudson, N.Y.: Anthroposophic Press.

About the Authors

Cheryl Sanders, Ph.D. is co founder of the School of Spiritual Psychology, and an addiction counselor and teacher, having worked in public agencies and private practice for 18 years. She co-founded a program in Perinatal Intervention at Parkland Hospital, Dallas, and conducts workshops on forming community coalitions for women and minority groups for health and human services. She also conducts workshops for faculties and parents dealing with teaching about abuse, violence, and addictive behaviors. The care of the senses is her primary research work. (Cheryl died in 2015)

Robert Sardello, Ph.D. is co founder of the School of Spiritual Psychology.

He has served as the director of the undergraduate and graduate programs in phenomenological psychology at the University of Dallas, and as Director of the Institute of Philosophic Studies there. He, along with his wife, Cheryl, has presented in workshops and conferences throughout the United States as well as well as multiple times in

Cheryl Sanders Sardello, &Robert Sardello,

Canada, England, Australia, Ireland, and the Philippines, He is one of the founders of the Dallas Institute of Humanities and Culture. He has published eight books and many monographs.

Acknowledgment

Much gratitude to Dr. Scott Scribner for his careful reading of the manuscript of this monograph, and for his extensive editorial work with it.

Made in United States
North Haven, CT
09 January 2022

14400955R00052